The classroom caterpillars

Story by Dawn McMillan   **Illustrations by Meredith Thomas**

On Friday morning,

Katie came to school

with a caterpillar in a box.

She had some leaves in the box, too.

Katie said to Miss Park,

"I will look after this caterpillar.

Can it stay here in our room?"

"My caterpillar likes eating
green leaves," said Katie.

Miss Park said,
"Look under this leaf.
Here are some little white eggs.
Tiny caterpillars will come out
of the eggs."

On Monday morning,
Katie came to school
with a green plant in a pot.

"Look!" she said to Anna.
"Some little caterpillars
have come out of the eggs!
They can eat this plant, too."

All that week, and the next week,
the tiny caterpillars nibbled
at the plant leaves.

The caterpillars got bigger
and bigger and **bigger**!
They nibbled more
and more leaves!

"Look at the plant now!" said Katie.

"The leaves are all gone!
We have no more plants
for them to eat."

"Oh, **no**!" said Anna.

"The caterpillars are still hungry!"

"Caterpillars will eat pumpkin,"
said Miss Park.

"I can get some pumpkin
from home," said Katie.

The little caterpillars
liked eating the pumpkin.
But Katie's big caterpillar
was not hungry any more.
It was under a leaf.

"My caterpillar is making a **chrysalis**,"
said Katie.

"It's going to be a butterfly one day," said Anna.